I0112216

A KINDNESS MANIFESTO

A Kindness Manifesto

JOHN LAMY

LYNX PUBLISHERS

Copyright © 2025 by John Lamy.

ISBN (eBook/Kindle): 978-1-968012-34-2

ISBN (Paperback): 978-1-968012-35-9

Library Of Congress Catalog Card Number: 2025920480

All rights reserved. No part of this book may be reproduced or transmitted in any form or by any means, electronic or mechanical, including photocopying, recording, or by any information storage and retrieval system without express written permission from the author, except in the case of brief quotations embodied in critical reviews and certain other noncommercial uses permitted by copyright law.

Published in the United States of America by Lynx Publishers.

DEDICATION

To my wife Gail and my son Patrick.

Thank you for your boundless love, support, and kindness over all these years.

TABLE OF CONTENTS

The Big Idea 9

The Context 13

The Problems 15

The Solution 24

Capitalism..42

Examples..48

Summary 51

Thanks and Acknowledgments 54

A Personal Request...55

Meet the Author 56

THE BIG IDEA

We've got problems. Big problems. Some of them threaten our very existence. Not only are we not getting them solved, we're losing ground every day.

Einstein said, "We cannot solve our problems with the same thinking we used when we created them." It looks to me like we're proving him right at every turn.

Recall the iceberg metaphor. Our problems are on the surface, where we can see them:

- Climate change
- Nuclear war
- Artificial Intelligence run amok
- Gutting our science & research
- Racism
- Global decline of Democracy
- Economic inequality
- Homelessness
- Gun violence
- Wars: irrational, almost medieval
- On and on... You know the story.

Here's the thing: the root causes of these problems are *below the surface*. They're the bigger bulk of the iceberg that we can't see directly. Every one of these highly visible problems traces back to the more invisible human interior: our thoughts, feelings, emotions, and intentions. These interior factors drive human behavior and culture, which in turn drive our problems.

If we have any hope of solutions, we're going to have to, for the first time in human history, excavate this interior landscape on a grand scale.

We've tried solutions founded on rationality, our head. We quantify things, we pursue economics and material factors...very rational. But rationality is what triggered the problems in the first place. Einstein says, "Gotta go deeper!" It's time to go below the surface of the iceberg, to invoke the *heart*, the wiser and more powerful organ. As you well know, the interior landscape is vast and profound, filled with memories, traumas, old hurts and resentments, emotional reactions, compulsions; and with hopes and dreams, desires and longings, compassion and love for other people, a feeling of interconnection with all life, a sense of vision and hope for a truly livable and loving world. These are the forces that render our culture inclusive or alienating, and that will ultimately decide our survival.

And we connect with those powerful forces through our *heart*, not just our head. Establishing that deep heart connection and working through it involves a major personal commitment. And there is a path that connects these two levels, the surface and the interior, that you can embark on immediately, that can help you navigate your own interior and at the same time materially contribute to solution to the surface problems. That path is *kindness*.

On the interior level, you'll find that practicing kindness invites you to take a look at your feelings about other people. That opens the door to what's really going on inside, and it's step one in developing a healthy interior life.

On the exterior level, the recipients of your kindness can relax their uptightness just a bit, they can let down and be a little more human and real. Less need for defensiveness. Less need for a nuclear weapon.

The effects of kindness are cumulative. It works like yeast as it expands through a baking loaf of bread. It works like ripples on a pond. It moves. It touches people as it goes, and they touch others. In its quiet way, kindness is extremely powerful.

I visualize kindness building up on four levels: personal, cultural, business, and government, each building on the last.

It's time for us to collectively heed Einstein's advice. We don't *eliminate* the rational, but we add to it by opening our hearts, and by generating actions in the external world based on positive, life-affirming interior feelings. That's *kindness*. And the cumulative impact of a mass wave of kindness is the power to solve our problems.

I don't see anything else on the horizon that can do that.

PAUSE AND REVIEW QUESTION: How do you feel about the idea that going deeper, moving from just the head to including the heart, can open the door to solutions to our big problems? Does that really sound right to you? How so?

THE CONTEXT

I look out at the world these days and sometimes feel overwhelmed, sorrowful, and a little hopeless. Sure, there's plenty of good news out there, but sometimes it feels like Dickens' "Worst of Times," as though darkness is enveloping the planet. Do you ever feel like that?

I heard some good advice recently: limit your intake of really bad news, and then find *one place* where you can genuinely contribute to the solutions.

That's why I'm writing this. I feel like we have a profound solution to our darkening world, it's right here in front of us, and it's always been there. It's just that it's never been widely put into practice. Now more than ever, we need a radical breakthrough. This manifesto is a suggestion for that breakthrough. It's something we can all do that will help. Something that can offer realistic hope.

This book is geared for thoughtful people, people predisposed to action, from the whole range of political persuasions, from both sides of the aisle.

Folks who are more committed to solving our problems than just hawking their philosophy.

We seriously need a breakthrough, and this just might be it!

THE PROBLEMS

Here's where we start going deeper.

Each problem has its own set of causes. Most of these causes are complex, and they operate on many levels at the same time. Smart people are working hard to unravel that vast network of causes, but they're mostly stuck at the rational level. So they seem to be making very little progress, if any.

But here's what's different: we can also identify a small number of *underlying* causes that strongly influence many, if not most, of our big problems. This is not a *simplification*; it's a deeper dive that includes, but goes beyond, the detailed network of proximate, rational causes. This is moving into the submerged part of the iceberg, the interior landscape that's largely invisible.

What follows is a small slice from that interior landscape, just to get an idea of how it works and how you might feel your way into it. I've picked what I think are the biggest contributors to our surface problems, human aspects that we all share and can all work on.

Individuality

Many insightful observers, starting with de Tocqueville, have noted that the US embodies a disproportionate share of *individuality* in our national outlook. That individuality has been a major key to our country's astonishing success. I experience it in my own personal life, and I observed it vividly in my years working in Silicon Valley. And in my travels abroad, I've seen individuality at work virtually universally. It feels like an aspect of being human.

Individuality is a compelling component of our problems, but it's also critical that we preserve the healthy part of that individuality as we go forward.

Interconnection: Lost Awareness

Somewhere deep in the American psyche is a panorama of wide-open spaces, the great primaeval prairie, the cowboy loping along under the endless sky. That image nurtures our predisposition toward individuality, and I think similar images play out all around the world. But unfortunately that tasty image leaves out a fundamental reality of life: our *interconnection* with all of life and the entirety of existence. The power of cause and effect is always at work, and we're both causers and receivers of effects.

Awareness of interconnection means we keep our eyes open, we study our total environment, and we cultivate an attitude of care and stewardship toward that living whole. We feel ourselves not as separate but as part of the whole, and we act accordingly.

In a healthy person and a healthy culture, individuality and awareness of interconnection work together in a dynamic balance: I assert myself, but I also observe other people and my environment, and I'm mindful of my impact on them. That delicate balance is inherently sustainable, but it doesn't come for free. We have to nurture it, to cultivate it, especially our awareness of interconnection. Unfortunately, that cultivation has faded in our culture.

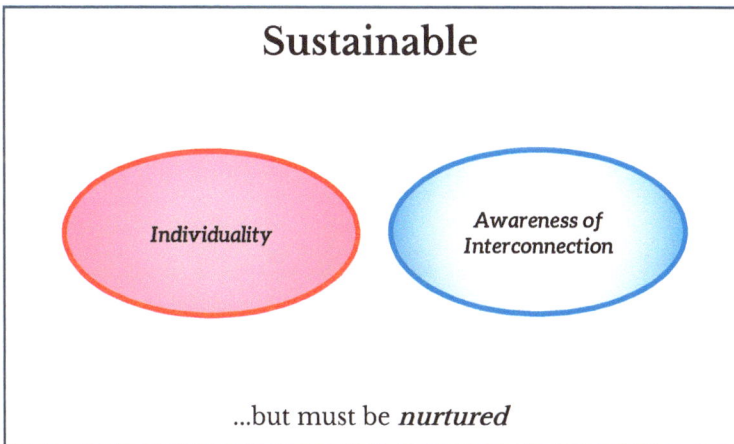

Sustainable

Individuality

Awareness of Interconnection

...but must be ***nurtured***

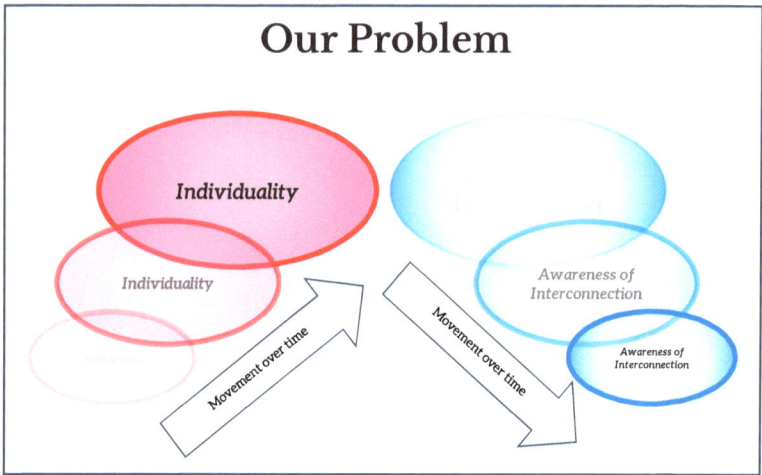

Our Problem

Individuality

Individuality

Movement over time

Movement over time

Awareness of Interconnection

Awareness of Interconnection

In recent decades, we've afforded ourselves the luxury of mostly *ignoring* interconnection. We tend not to pay attention to our impact on other people, on our immediate systems, and on the planet as a whole. For example, if I drive from my home in Oregon to Los Angeles in my gasoline-powered car, I put 500 pounds of CO_2 into the air. That CO_2 raises the earth's temperature by a tiny amount... my personal contribution to global warming.

Another example, maybe at work we use the solvent Trichloroethylene to clean parts. When it gets dirty, we just pour it into the little creek behind the factory. The people downstream who get their water from wells contract cancer at a much higher rate than normal.

We've gotten away with ignoring interconnection partly because we've been so abundantly endowed with resources, open spaces, two oceans, etc. But ignoring interconnection is a serious cause of our problems.

Consumption

An important by-product of Individuality is that we tend to consume without much constraint. We take from the earth and from each other, more or less without thinking about it. It feels like more is better, so that's what we do.

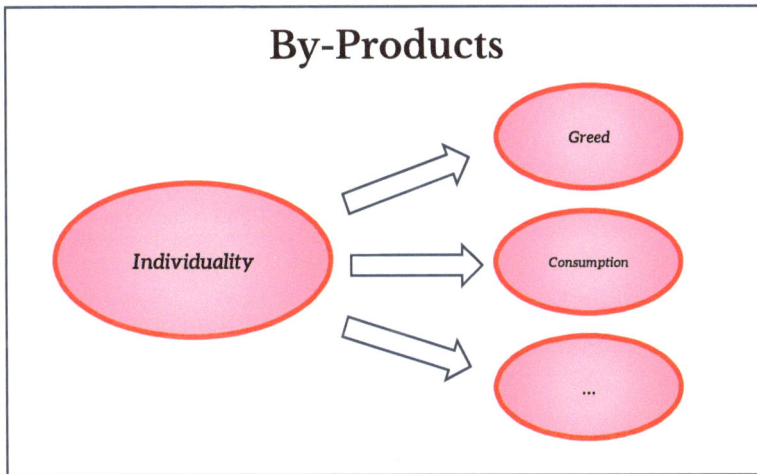

By-Products

Individuality → Greed

Individuality → Consumption

Individuality → ...

If you go to a world fact book and look up a specific country, the first metric you'll see is the country's per capita Gross Domestic Product, and its growth. And that metric is the primary figure politicians pay attention to. What is GDP? Basically, it's a measure of what we produce and consume. And our national goal is to grow it forever. So we've built this colossal industrial/commercial machine, replete with omnipresent promotion and advertising, that drives us to consume more and more.

We rarely face the question, "How much is enough?" We think we don't have to face that question. We act as if there are no meaningful constraints on our consumption.

But now, in 2025, we're finding that there *are* constraints. First and foremost, the planet can only supply a finite amount of *stuff*, and can only absorb a finite amount of our cast-off. And we've discovered that our CO_2 emissions will very soon kill us through global warming. The same goes for other consumption-originated emissions. You know the story.

But even closer to home, therapists' offices are packed with people who thought their big house, nice car, and great vacations would make them happy. But they woke up one day and found themselves troubled nonetheless. I've fallen into that illusion a time or two myself. It turns out that consumption confers happiness for a while, but it wears off pretty quickly. Have you noticed that in your life?

Imbalance

These three factors—Individuality, Lost Awareness of Interconnection, and Consumption—have been aggregating over the decades in the US. Today, we've reached a tipping point where their impact is suddenly triggering massive problems.

It's been a gradual, slow *eclipsing of our awareness of interconnectedness*, combined with a growing reluctance to nurture it. We've let our awareness of macro-level Cause and Effect quietly slip into the background as so many great technological solutions seem to mitigate the effects of our actions, and to provide distraction, and even entertainment, to lure our attention away from our interconnection.

In sum: *We've lost the balance between individuality and interconnection.* That loss is starting to kill us.

Look back at that list of problems. Can you see how this loss of balance has contributed materially to each of them? For example, economic inequality. Since you're reading this book, you probably have a decent job and a fairly steady income, a serviceable home and car, all the trappings. You work hard, and you rightly take credit for your situation. You continually scan the horizon for opportunities that might further enhance your life.

But how often do you think about, or even notice, those 35 million people in the US (the 11% in "poverty") who don't have what you have? Or *feel* how it feels to live with their continual insecurity...if their old clunker doesn't start tomorrow, it's bye-bye job. Do you unconsciously attribute their situation to laziness or character weakness, versus your own hard work and rectitude? How often do you truly acknowledge the massive role of *good luck* in your life and *lousy luck* in theirs?

If this is you, even to some extent, then your individuality and hard work are big assets and important parts of your mindset, but your *awareness of their situation* has not kept up. It's atrophied almost to the point of being inconsequential. It's out of balance, it's unable to throttle back the growing elitism and hardness of heart that can accompany untethered individuality. And growing economic inequality is one of the deeply caustic dysfunctions we're living with right now.

And that's just one example from a big list of problems.

PAUSE AND REVIEW QUESTION: When in your life have you had a personal/emotional experience of your connection to the larger life? To other people who aren't quite like you, to the fullness of nature, to the planet as a whole? It's reported that many of us occasionally have these soul-touching experiences; how about you?

THE SOLUTION

The Solution will have to operate on four levels at the same time: Personal, Cultural, Business, and Governmental. And obviously each level will need to build on the one below it. So... our personal commitment is critical to getting anything done. Don't underestimate your personal impact!

Interconnection

Interconnection is where the most fundamental rebalancing needs to happen. While preserving our unique individuality, we need to greatly enhance our awareness of other people and other entities, and our impact on them. This awareness is mostly a matter of how much attention we devote to people and events outside of ourselves. It's a deeply personal dynamic, often the outcome of personal analysis, reflection and interior work...at least that's how it's been for me.

Kindness

As we begin to dig into the deeper realms of the submerged part of the iceberg, where the real but mostly unnoticed causes of our problems originate, we discover an interesting and helpful phenomenon. There is a powerful two-way connection between awareness of interconnection and kindness.

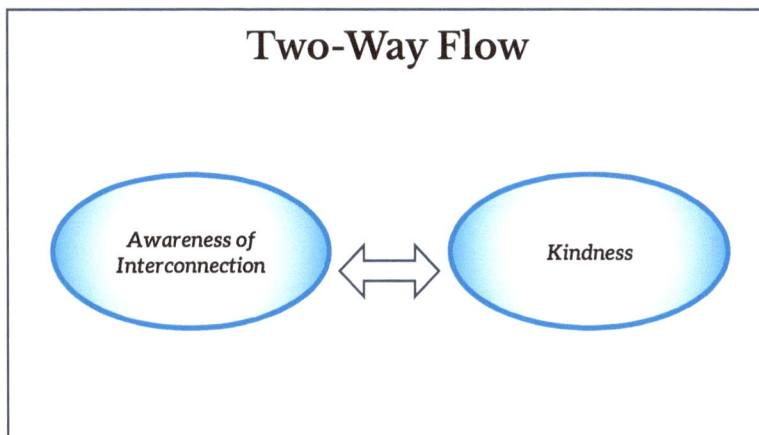

Two-Way Flow

Awareness of Interconnection ⟺ Kindness

First, from awareness of interconnection to kindness. It seems fairly obvious that, as we become aware of other people and begin to care for them, we would naturally respond with kindness. We'd reach out, we'd help them where we can. If you're at a party and somebody suddenly collapses with a heart attack, you'd call a doctor right away. And you'd do that even if the victim's politics were opposite to yours—you just would! Kindness follows awareness. It just does!

But how about the other way, from kindness to awareness of interconnection? Not quite as obvious. What if you make a serious commitment to kindness as a daily practice. Key: that commitment, in and of itself, will inspire a scanning of the horizon for a place to *practice* your kindness. You'll begin to look around with new eyes: "I'm a part of all this. Where can I help?" If you're like me, your commitment will organically nurture a new *interior quiet* and *curiosity* that you might not have experienced before. Within that framework, a new awareness can arise. You begin to see connections you just skimmed over before, and you begin to have heartfelt compassion for needful situations. You'll naturally want to jump in and help.

Personal example: Over the past six months, I've deliberately cut back on being busy. No more big list every day, like I'd done for decades. So now there's time for reading, thinking, and meditating that wasn't there before. And for reading to kids (below) and writing Manifestos!

Friends of mine had talked about how capitalism has gradually morphed into a harmful influence, so I began to think and write about that, drawing from my MBA and consulting background. I felt like I was in a unique position to contribute thoughts that might help. As I beavered away on this little project, which a few weeks earlier wasn't even a glimmer of an idea! — It occurred that out-of-control capitalism was just *one of many* big problems, and that the solution was deeper than most of what you read about (thinking of Einstein). So right now, as I sit here typing, I feel like I'm moving into territory that's very much unknown to me, but that may have real potential to help.

All this because a while back I'd made a commitment to what I call "loving kindness," without even knowing where it would go. The interconnection I hadn't thought about was with *you*, a potential reader who wants to help out and who might appreciate a little concrete thinking on the subject.

To summarize this second flow, kindness to awareness of interconnection:

- Commit to kindness in your life;
- Gently scan the horizon for places where your personal superpower might contribute;
- Allow a quietude, an openness, a curiosity... an empty space where new things can flow in;
- When you find such a place, jump in and give it your all;
- Then be willing to make changes as you go, to adapt to what the world is telling you is working and not working.

Kindness and Interconnection

Truth is, we need both flows to solve our problems. And they work together and nurture each other. So it doesn't really matter which one you start with, because starting with either one will lead to the other in time.

Awareness of interconnection is critically essential, but it's quieter. It's within your mind and heart. Kindness is more active; it manifests in the world out there. It's a direct expression of your awareness of your interconnections. So at the end of the day, to truly solve our problems, we'll need the active expression of kindness out there in the world.

Slippery Slope

Warning! There's a slippery slope here. Remember how your mom told you, "Be nice to Billy, and he'll be nice to you?" That's often true enough, but that's not what we're talking about here. That type of "kindness" is called *transactional*, and it's actually more of an *investment* that you hope will pay you back...so we're back to an opportunity for my individuality and benefit to myself. The kindness we're talking about here is given totally freely, with zero strings attached and no expectations on the outcome. The only "payback" is to the whole system, to the reduction of the world's problems.

The genuine kindness I'm describing almost always goes beyond math and logic, and actually involves an element of *paradox*. Real kindness means *giving*: maybe it's money, maybe it's your precious time and attention. You'll have a little bit less in your pocket than you would without your kind act.

But wait: maybe not! Maybe your kindness, compounded with others' kindness, causes the *whole system* to heal itself and to benefit everyone...including you! As wise people over the millennia have said, in order to really *live*, something in you has to *die*. It's sometimes called *The Great Paradox*.

Two examples. My high school math teacher used to give me a few extra problems that were outside the normal curriculum...hard problems! Over time, those problems expanded my mastery of math and enabled me to get into a top engineering school, and feel comfortable with math my whole life. Just doing his job?? It felt like *way beyond* that, a true kindness that I can only return by paying it forward.

Second example. For about five years, my wife and a handful of her friends planted trees in Santa Rosa, CA. The kindness was simple: trees absorb CO_2, they provide shade, and they enhance the total environment. Before long, their little team had grown to a formal organization called Global ReLeaf (get it?!), and they planted thousands of trees in Sonoma County. Their kindness resulted in CO_2 reduction and urban beautification, and maybe more importantly, in broad education about climate change and the fact that we can make a difference.

Finally, please take a look at the truly kind people in your circle. I suspect you'll find them more fulfilled and more alive than the people who calculate every move, looking for self-preservation and self-aggrandizement.

The Four Levels

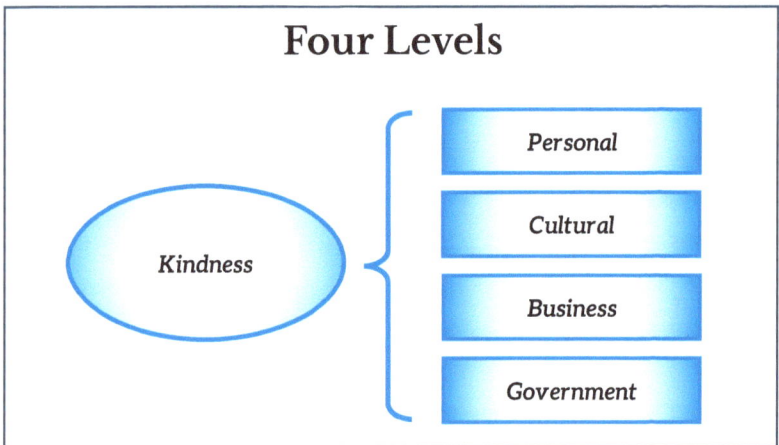

Four Levels

Kindness

- Personal
- Cultural
- Business
- Government

PERSONAL

Personal kindness works in two domains: individual and larger scale.

Individual kindness starts with little things. Tiny but frequent anonymous acts, beneficial to folks in your immediate circle. Warmth. Genuine interest in what they have to say. All of this helps people relax, feel less stressed out, and to be less prone to subtle defensiveness.

Start with that. You already do it, just do more. Make it habitual.

And then: pick *one* bigger thing that involves a commitment of your personal time and attention, something that resonates with your superpower and your interests. Something that truly helps on a bigger scale. My wife and I are involved with a reading program at a local elementary school that serves a less affluent community. She manages the program, and I'm one of the volunteer readers. We love it! And so do the kids. And those kids experience a significant and measurable lift in their academic performance...it truly helps!

And realize that anything you do to help tackle environmental problems and global warming is a profound kindness—to other people, to other generations, and to the planet itself.

And importantly, when you're exercising kindness like this, don't forget to give off vibes of fun and humor! Don't mope around like a martyr. Add cheer and energy and joie de vivre to your environment. Be the one who says "Yes!" In truth, that in itself is a profound kindness.

My friend Frank De Luca wrote this poem. It feels so appropriate as we begin to practice the personal dimension of kindness:

COMPASSION

I did not know
That the rude sales clerk's son
Was just expelled from school

I did not know
That the careless driver who pulled out in front of me
Just got the call that his father had died

I did not know
That my sarcastic remark
Had hurt my friend so deeply

I do know
That I easily forget

How tender we all are

I do know
That erring on the side of kindness
Never hurt a soul

Frank De Luca
© June 2015, all rights reserved
Used by permission

My suggestion: seriously consider making kindness a fundamental part of your own personal operating system. You'll give the world, and yourself, a huge lift.

CULTURAL

We can observe the utter failure of the purely cerebral, head-only approach in our study of *culture*. Culture is clearly a heart thing, a values thing; to exclude the heart dimension in examining culture is to ensure failure.

A vivid example is Thomas Frank's landmark *"What's the Matter with Kansas?"* published in 2004. Frank points out that lower income Midwest conservatives tend to vote against their economic self-interest. The coastal elites often look at that situation with disdain and scorn, and of course those Midwest folks feel their snobbery and superiority and rebel against it. Result: a bitterly divided culture that, today, is bordering on non-functional.

Example: those elites have a tendency to think that money can solve most of the problems associated with generational poverty and crime, but it just hasn't worked. Money is necessary, but even more important is the value structure, the personal characteristics, of the parents as they raise their kids. Those human dimensions get obliterated in purely quantitative studies, so the resulting corrective initiatives tend to fail.

What to do? Let's use "kindness" as a shorthand for a range of positive, supportive emotions. We can start by *noticing*, as I personally have to my great shock and embarrassment, those times when we disdain and scorn folks whose values and actions we deem to be inferior to our own. We look down our noses...and make no mistake, they *feel* it!

When you catch yourself doing that, launch kindness: shut up and truly listen, work hard to understand what they are feeling and thinking, even if you initially disagree with it. Just understand and feel.

Then, muster up respect for them. If you're thinking clearly, their position almost always has *some* merit, it adds some value to the overall situation. For example, liberals who want to make changes and improvements will have to admit that, well yes, there are some parts of the old existing order that we do actually value and that we should keep. Let's be careful not to toss the baby with the bathwater.

Doing that is kind. Doing that will help to heal the rift that has battered our culture in the last couple of decades.

And, the truth is that doing that is not easy. We are so programmed to respond to these situations *reactively, compulsively*. Fortunately there's a strategic tool that has proven effective again and again, that makes it all a lot easier: when we get triggered, just *pause*. Literally *stop* for about five seconds. Let yourself settle down, and then deliberately shift away from the *Let Me Tell You* mode and into the *Deep Listening* mode.

The other thing at work here: don't forget self-kindness, also called self-compassion. As you allow more and more kindness in your life, you'll stumble over your own flaws and shortcomings. Our superego wants to beat us up about that; I'm saying, *don't go there*. It's actually not healthy to inflict that kind of violence (yes!) on yourself. Realize that you're just a human being trying to be kind toward others on our shared planet, and you don't always get it perfect the first time!

What I'm describing here are some of the deeper dynamics that accompany a commitment to kindness as a way of life, as part of your total operating system. It's an opening to your own personal life's journey, and it can bring you a fullness and depth of experience, or maybe an expansion of your life's horizons, that might be new.

----- ----- ----- ----- ----- ----- -----

A friend told me something profound he learned in his graduate work at MIT: we can't always agree on *values*, but even so, we *can* agree on a *shared course of action*. I find this idea extremely helpful as we contemplate how to inspire cross-political collaboration in the face of our monumental problems. This principle applies especially at the next two levels.

BUSINESS

I know people who say we should totally get rid of capitalism, that it's the root cause of most of our problems. Capitalism is often driven by greed (the worst face of individualism). Capitalism, including massive advertising and promotion, has stimulated enormous consumption of resources, plus waste and pollution. We can't keep going on the track we're on... but *get rid of it*?? Hmmm...not so sure. (See a later section for more on capitalism.)

Two problems: First, capitalism, with its Invisible Hand, has actually done an excellent job on the *supply* side (meaning the allocation of resources for production, and the use of pricing as a signal). The key to capitalism is this: a business *must make a profit* at the end of the day. Losses year after year tell us that either the product isn't truly attractive to customers, or that the producer can't build it efficiently enough to price it attractively. Capitalism's signal: close the business.

Second, whatever we replace capitalism with would involve a *planning* apparatus to replace the Invisible Hand to allocate resources. That apparatus has been shown time and again to be inefficient, cumbersome, and prone to corruption. My wife and I visited the Soviet Union in the 80s, and I can attest to the grief their system visited upon its citizens. I remember a hot summer day and a long line of kids clambering for ice cream. There was only one person behind the counter, sleepily scooping cones. Poor planning, poor incentivization. We don't want that.

So our strategy needs to be this: retain capitalism, but fix the parts that are broken and that contribute to our list of problems. That would include especially the distribution and consumption side. The lists below have a few example ideas for how to actually implement kindness in business. And here are a few more ideas and examples:

Businesses could refine and expand their role in the community. Encourage their employees to be coaches and mentors in their hometowns. Hold open houses and tours. Sponsor internships. Planning could put more emphasis on the long term, and not just the next quarter. Our near-religious worship of growth could be throttled back to include accommodation of the carrying capacity of the earth itself. Maybe slower growth is ok if there are huge benefits...which there are!

And finally, an individual business could nurture kindness as a fundamental aspect of its culture. Yes, it might take a bite out of today's profit. But that bite might be offset by the benefit to the community as a whole.

A personal example that really spoke to me: six months ago, I bought a fairly expensive backpack at REI...it looked great! Then I used it on a trip and...it wasn't so great after all. In fact, I just plain didn't like it. So I took it back to the store, and I was totally amazed at how kindly they treated me. Though it had been used on a trip, they took it back no problem, gave me a full refund, and didn't make me feel like a jerk. I came away feeling like I'd been treated with total kindness and respect. That transaction probably cost them a few hundred dollars, but today I'm a total REI promoter and I talk about them enthusiastically whenever I can. I am advertising that you just can't buy! And notice that this is more than being nice to Billy; it's doing the kind thing with zero control of what the customer will do.

GOVERNMENT

Finally, the highest leverage and most challenging arena for kindness is government. Challenging because governments are rightly expected to practice "fiduciary responsibility," meaning their expenditures need to make sense. And "make sense" means different things to people of different political and cultural persuasions.

The thing is, if we can genuinely implement kindness in our government, then we'll go a long way toward solving that list of problems. We'd ask, what programs are truly beneficial to the greatest good? We'd seriously study interdependence and get away from just making the lobbyist-powered entities better off.

When the discussion moves into government, the subject of welfare fraud usually pops up. Yes, it's out there. Research says around 4% to 7% of recipients will cheat. OK, let's work on that, but let's not let those folks ruin it for the whole population. There are, in fact, a lot of people who aren't as lucky as you and I are, and who truly need help. Kindness says, let's help them. Liberals and conservatives should work together on building the systems, while avoiding the impulse to beat up the other side and have their own philosophy win out. The Scandinavian countries, and others, have done a pretty good job...let's learn from them and then go from there.

The discussion in a later section includes several possible government initiatives. I visualize these initiatives as the outcome of discussion and negotiation among the differing interests. I mentioned earlier, differing values but a shared course of action. These programs need to be the product of compromise and reasonableness, and not just mindless allegiance to political dogma and endless bullying.

And here's a great suggestion for making that negotiation process a little easier. What if every year, at tax time, the taxpayers could designate how they would like the *elective* portion of their taxes spent? That is, some expenditures are basically predetermined (defense, social security, highways, etc.), but a significant part of federal expenditure goes to programs that reflect our *values* (foreign aid, welfare, scientific research, etc.). Check a box or give a percentage to indicate your personal support. It would be like voting, not every two or four years but every year, and voting directly for what you want, not just for a representative. You can begin to see the benefits on multiple levels.

PAUSE AND REVIEW QUESTION: Think back over the past few days in your life; when did you do something kind for somebody? How did that go? How did you feel? How did they feel? Can you imagine doing more of that? And can you imagine scaling it up to take on a project compatible with your values and your superpowers that is fundamentally based on kindness, and not generating benefit for yourself?

CAPITALISM

Capitalism deserves a little extra treatment because it's so globally pervasive, and because it's clearly one of the major causes of our big problems.

But there's much more to it than that. Capitalism has brought us so many benefits, and it's part of our *solution* as well. Capitalism is often regarded as antithetical to kindness... the two seem like natural enemies. So my job here will be to *reconcile* them.

Capitalism and economics are obviously huge, complicated subjects, so I'm going summarize this discussion into three simple lists that outline strengths, weaknesses, and solutions. I'll go light on details, but mostly cover the waterfront.

And mainly I'll show how kindness itself can offset most of capitalism's weaknesses. Capitalism and economics are built on a framework of mathematics and logic, and, thinking back to Einstein's dictum, that's where the problems begin. To solve the problems we'll have to go to the deeper level, one which accommodates values and feelings and the whole human dimension. Namely, kindness.

Strengths of Capitalism

- Efficient allocation of resources. Adam Smith's Invisible Hand does a great job at moving investments around to meet our economic needs without any central planning. Entrepreneurs simply do what seems in their own best interest, and the rest (mostly!) takes care of itself.
- Encouragement of innovation and technical progress. Think iPhone, defibrillator, automobile, on and on.
- Availability of wide choices and reasonable prices for consumers. We vote with our dollars, and companies respond.
- Rapid adaptability and flexibility. Remember how quickly companies responded to COVID?
- Globally improved standard of living. Poverty rates are way down worldwide, thanks in large measure to global capitalism.

Weaknesses of Capitalism

- Environmental destruction.
- Externalities: costs that aren't reflected in the company's financials or the pricing of the final product. Those externalized costs are usually absorbed by the government or someone else

besides the company. Examples include pollution and natural resource depletion. Externalities are a major contribution to environmental destruction, above.

- Extreme inequality.
- Short term thinking.
- Job loss and hollowing out of capabilities due to globalization.
- Obsession with growth, without much or any awareness of natural limits. Unfettered growth is also supported by externalities.
- Monetization of everything. For example, we treat the earth as a *thing*, a resource to be exploited. Traditional reverence and love for the earth tend to take a back seat, with huge negative consequences, on many levels.

Suggestions for Improvement

As we mentioned earlier, I'm not in favor of scrapping capitalism. The alternatives, especially those requiring lots of centralized planning, have been shown over and over not to work very well (remember those Russian kids waiting for their ice cream?).

Same goes for David Ricardo's idea of globalization based on "comparative advantage," meaning everybody wins if we focus on what we do best; but we do have to acknowledge the serious impact of job loss, and do a much better job with that than we've done so far.

These improvements will require the sincere involvement of both liberals and conservatives in building systems to mitigate the weaknesses and problems. That's a very tall order, and we've not done well at it so far; we're losing our ability to collaborate and to compromise. "Compromise" has become a four-letter word, unfortunately. By its very nature it moves beyond logic, and therefore into the territory of real solutions as implied by Einstein. You'll see kindness at every step of the way in the following list of suggestions for improving capitalism.

- Stakeholder-based strategy. This approach is also called People, Planet, Profit. It includes the interests of *all* the major stakeholders, including:
  o Owners/shareholders, the traditional main beneficiaries of an enterprise
  o Employees
  o Customers
  o Suppliers
  o The Community
  o The total environment, the planet

- Market mechanisms to address externalities. Also called pricing in the real costs. Examples:
  - Carbon tax
  - Tax or outright fees for pollution
  - Incentives for renewables
  - Subsidies for sustainable practices
- Broad-scale electrification with renewable sources. Examples:
  - Solar and wind power, with battery storage
  - Electric Vehicles
  - Heat pumps
  - Smart grid
- Adoption of metrics alternative to GDP Growth.
- Mandatory disclosures, for example:
  - Climate risk factors
  - Resource use
  - Pollution
  - Externalities
- Stronger social safety nets and meeting universal needs, for example:
  - Healthcare
  - Education
  - Worker protection
- Retraining programs for workers with offshored jobs
- Sustainable land use policies

- Housing and zoning regulations that accommodate the need for adequate numbers of homes at reasonable prices

In what way do every one of these suggestions incorporate kindness? Because each one goes beyond a simple short-term return on investment calculation, and folds in longer term *values* that address the real needs of real people. My contention is that doing so will make many more people happy with their lives, give them more equal access to opportunities, and build a stronger overall culture. And in the end, save the earth from the suicidal path that we're currently pursuing. I'm pretty sure most intelligent and well-intended people of any political persuasion would say YES to that.

PAUSE AND REVIEW QUESTION: Do you honestly think there's room for kindness in capitalism? How might that work on your job?

EXAMPLES

Here are a few more ideas to help get your mind churning!

PERSONAL

- **Volunteer** with Big Brothers Big Sisters or similar organizations.
- Be kind when you're **driving**. Let people cut in. Stop for crossing pedestrians. Don't zoom in and out on the freeway. You know the drill... just mellow out a bit behind the wheel.
- If you have money, **donate** to worthy causes, especially local ones. Cultivate involvement with those local charities, help steer them. Often, the smaller locals need the money more than the larger, big-name charities. And you may be able to lend a much-appreciated perspective and leadership.

CULTURAL

- Catch yourself being **judgmental** of folks whose values don't really measure up to yours; and switch into the *careful listen* mode immediately. Make yourself understand and feel their perspective.

BUSINESS

- As mentioned above, businesses explicitly include their **stakeholders** in their strategy. Many leading businesses are beginning to do this, and business schools are beginning to teach it.
- Take on **day-long group projects** in your community, like having a team from a department clean a beach or plant trees. This approach stimulates a sense of ownership for your community, which is sometimes lacking between a company and its surrounding town.

GOVERNMENT

- Identify the unintended consequences of **regulations** and work to balance their beneficial and undesirable impacts. Many important and highly contributory projects are delayed and run over budget because we didn't think through the downsides of regulation. We need regulations, but let's get them back into balance. Think of the possible impacts on *everybody*.
- In politics, attack the ideas, policies, and proposals, but not the person and their character. Stop the emotional *vitriol* that's so infected our politics in recent decades. Yes, statistically, **attack ads** work.

But that's only because we allow them to. We can vote against politicians who routinely use them.

SUMMARY

Our massive problems are starting to boil over. Sometimes it feels hopeless. The world is *calling out* for some kind of a profound change.

I think the solution is at hand!

What do our big problems share in common? Our deep-seated image of ourselves as *individuals* has gradually grown out of balance with our natural sense of *interconnection* with each other, with all of nature, and with the planet as a whole. Self-gratifying consumption has come to dominate our cultural landscape, and awareness of other people and our impacts on them, and on the whole system, has atrophied to the point of inconsequence.

What can we do? Step one: deliberately expand our awareness beyond our own immediate self, to include others and the whole system. This may involve personal work, meditation, group interactions, and lots of things.

Step two, and here's the key: Take explicit action to contribute to them and their well-being. It's called kindness. Many small acts of kindness every day. A few serious, deliberate initiatives that take real effort and attention on your part, or that of your culture, your company, or your legislature.

Guidelines:

- Start with noticing other people and their challenges, and/or start with an overall commitment to kindness in your life.
- Originate a kind action that will help someone else.
- Make it totally anonymous. No expectation of gain for yourself, even subtle ego-feel-good gain.
- Surrender all control of the outcome. We don't have much control over the outcome anyway, so just forget about it.
- Real kindness almost always transcends logic and calculation. If you truly give, you'll have a little less at the end of the day...
- ...Or, maybe the great paradox will kick in and the rising tide will lift all boats. That is my personal belief.

I postulate that profound, widespread kindness, operating at the level of the individual, the corporation, and the nation, has more than enough power to fix our problems and to change the world. Probably in ways that none of us could have imagined.

I see nothing else on the horizon that even comes close.

Let's give it a try! Think about it! This means *you*, dear reader!

This is Just a Start

There's obviously so much more to say about kindness. This Manifesto is really just a primer and an encouragement to take on kindness as a serious part of who you are. How do you really cultivate kindness? The Dalai Lama says, "Kindness is my religion." I interpret that to mean that a lot goes into the nurturing and development of genuine kindness. But still, if we just get started and go from there, I think we'll make a big difference.

PAUSE AND REVIEW QUESTION: How would you summarize this Manifesto in one or two sentences? Then, to what extent do you agree with it?

THANKS AND ACKNOWLEDGMENTS

So many of my friends have helped me with this project that I can't begin to list them all here. They've done it through conversations, reviews of early manuscripts, and just general ideation. I'm just thankful to have such wonderful friends!

And, my wife Gail stands out in her plowing through endless early versions and evolutions, and in the creative, insightful ideas she always brings to the table. Thank you Gail for the support and the substantive help!

A PERSONAL REQUEST

I hope to vigorously spread the idea of Kindness. And I want to ask your help in doing that. If this book has connected with you, please recommend it to your friends. I think your recommendation, along with the personal example of kindness in your life, may be the best way to bring active, effective kindness to our world.

Thank you!

MEET THE AUTHOR

I grew up in a small Midwestern town, as a Republican and a Catholic; I'm neither today. I have two younger brothers I'm still very close to. As a kid, I was a bit nerdy. I built a ham radio rig, a hi-fi, and lots of stuff like that. I got a degree in electrical engineering from MIT and went to work for a large Silicon Valley firm. Most of my 30 years there were as an engineering manager in R&D, and as a divisional quality manager. Mid-career, I got an MBA from Cornell and worked as a management consultant for 15 years.

Gail and I have been married for over 50 years. We have one grown son and one grandson in college, and I'm extremely proud of both of them. I've been a climate activist for decades. Over the years, our family has backpacked, skied, sailed, kayaked, biked, and traveled. We consider ourselves very, very fortunate.

I'm thankful these days that I have the time and the energy to work on projects like this Manifesto!

www.ingramcontent.com/pod-product-compliance
Lightning Source LLC
LaVergne TN
LVHW010028070426
835513LV00001B/19